RAISING SPARKS

RAISING SPARKS

Michael Symmons Roberts

CAPE POETRY

Published by Jonathan Cape 1999

2 4 6 8 10 9 7 5 3 1

ISBN 0-224-05902-5

Papers used by Random House UK Limited are natural,
recyclable products made from wood grown in sustainable forests.
The manufacturing processes conform to the environmental
regulations of the country of origin.

Typeset by Palimpsest Book Production Limited
Polmont, Stirlingshire

Printed and bound in Great Britain by
Creative Print and Design (Wales), Ebbw Vale

for Ruth

I have watched the wheels go round in case I might see the
living creatures like the appearance of lamps, in case I might see
the Living God projected from the Machine.

David Jones

There is in God (some say)
A deep, but dazzling darkness

Henry Vaughan

He dropped his voice & sybilled of
the death of the death of love.
I ought to get going.

John Berryman

CONTENTS

ACKNOWLEDGEMENTS

Acknowledgements are due to *Ambit, Arvon Poetry Competition Anthology, Independent, Leading Light, London Magazine, London Review of Books, National Poetry Competition Anthology, Nightwaves* (BBC Radio 3), *PN Review, Poetry Wales, Quadrant, Tempo, Third Way, Times Literary Supplement, Verse*

'Smithereens' was a collaboration with the composer James MacMillan, under the title 'Raising Sparks', commissioned as a song cycle by the Nash Ensemble with mezzo soprano Jean Rigby.

'Quickening' was also a collaboration with James MacMillan, a Proms choral commission by the Hilliard Ensemble and the BBC Symphony Chorus.

EXPECTING

There is another heart beating in this house,
another shoulder turning in the night.
Rain drips lost onto the unlit fire.
Gutters slowly clag with pasted leaves.
Quinces sharpen, shrivelling on their thorns
tended by the last few punch-drunk bees.
Maybe rain will slake the eucalyptus tree
whose desperate roots have undermined the house
and opened up an old crack in its face.
Somehow, from the summer's shallow sea,
a curl in the current was salvaged
and has grown into a miracle, a fish out of water,
looping and rolling through autumn and freeze.

FISH MOBILE

Alone as her child sleeps upstairs,
a mother sits in a sunlit window,
and contemplates how easy it is

to gut a marriage. Somewhere
in the muscle-memory, a knife
was kept sharp, and she had no idea

which one of them had used it,
or when. The varnished husks
of years that used to whip

through water circle slowly
in her mind. Sheen and scales remain,
but eyes dead and no tail-flick.

★

In a weatherbeaten house on the last
day of summer, a child lies awake
in his cot rehearsing language.

His 'O's and 'A's already make waves,
shaping the air above him,
sending the suspended shoal

round in a close mesmeric swim.
He knows where they came from,
this strange catch, from a distant

ocean where air had thickened up,
so lighter fish like these could cross
the thin seam from sea to sky.

Outside, hanging in clusters from trees
and walls are secret eggs of flying fish,
black and full, called elderberries.

CENTAUR

The story goes that when the war was won,
two men on horseback at either
side of Ypres could see each other
stamp and blow. No stone on stone
stood taller than a rider.

Even for an eyewitness, the image pales.
The clear line between man and mount
has blurred. Now, hands cupped to its mouth,
a hybrid clips across the debris,
crying like a shell-fall for its mate.

THE ADVENT HOUSE

We come in midwinter to a door
locked since August. Cold
has clenched the chair bones,
wall marrow. No firelighters,

logs damp and green. They spit
but will not catch. We breathe
on one strong spark, cosset it
with paper fists and kindling.

So much waits on it –
bluebottles and moths chilled
into stasis, a wounded king
in agony on the forest floor.

And if the fire fails: rain, rot,
and weed spores –
the patient seeds of wilderness.

SUN-DOGS

I first saw them at the end of an equatorial
summer, at full terrifying tilt across open fields

past a panic of birds; cattle weighted on dry grass.
Whatever animal the sun-dogs were after, their chase

must have ended in a kill, because that night
the thunder came, and then rain, and the drought

was finished – lying on its back against a shut gate
where it ran out of breath; its throat torn apart.

Domini canes; a pair, one white, one black,
guardians of order, watchdogs, custodians of luck.

I saw them leading when the beggars came to town,
like Sirius-twins at the feet of Orion;

other dogs – skin and bone on rope leads –
kept their distance, slept with men in makeshift beds;

men who wondered where these perfect strays
had come from, with such an amber in their eyes

and coats which, though immaculate in black and white,
became prismatic in the sun, too hot

to touch, as if they ever let you come that close.
They can start fires with the lick of a shadow;

expectant mothers brushed by them in dreams
know that their children will be famous

or anonymous, saints or beggars, or both.
Sometimes, like Tobias, Vitus, Roch, you feel a breath

on the back of each hand, and find them there.
One offers bread, part chewed, soft with saliva;

the other a punctured orange, sweet spittle
matting on the soft hair round its muzzle.

If you turn down the offerings, and shoo them,
they will go, and never come your way again.

If you eat they watch you, and you may discover
that bread tastes of manna, and orange of nectar.

Boundary-keepers, fire-masters, mock-suns;
they will sustain you then until your work is done.

FALL

The garden is cut and strung up;
Chinese Lanterns, Lavender, Honesty,
hang from the beams like carcasses.

All beliefs cast out, Descartes
turns his head above the fire to warm
his ghost. On the way to his slab table

– the unwritten book where he will find or lose it all –
his hair jags on dried flowers,
electric confetti peppers his back.

The clouds above his roof, urgent
all day to leave the world,
turn crystalline and fall as snow.

THE LUNG WASH

The first day, you cough up only water,
warm saline laced with vitamins and herbs.
Your lungs mistake healing for drowning,
they fetch up what tastes like the sea
into a white enamel bowl.
Your lungs mistake baptism for torture,
'O God, O my God, O God'.
You sought him out, like countless others
who speak too much and breathe too little,
you found the only doctor in the world
who washes lungs, and went to him.

The second day you know what comes –
'Breathe in Sir, now breathe out.'
The tube is pushed behind your voice
and water floods the hair's-breadth
channels of your lungs, you choke
'No no too much too much'
and phlegm rides up between the words,
coloured by the scent of home, and cigarettes.

By Wednesday the elegant office
with its dark red leather chairs
has won a terrifying fascination.
Sun streams through the window,
and the motes of dust light up
as if to show that air is only clean
when not seen for the carpet that it is.
Today you splutter up more phlegm,
with bonfires of your childhood,
other people's breath kissed into you,
incense and cooking smells
and long forgotten perfumes.

Then when all the phlegm is clear
the lighter, deeper hidden words begin
to bubble out into the room
'I always loved you, want to kill you,
be my life, come take my life.'

On Thursday morning you sleep in
and dream about a pulmonary specialist
in Venice with a plan, to counteract
the crumbling of his city with a thousand
human Venices, their lungs full
of the Grand Canal; but still you go.
'O Mama don't leave me, I'm hungry
I'm thirsty, I'm begging for some sleep'.
All the unsaid retches to be heard.
Il dottore with his bowl is ready to catch.

The last day you are growing into silence.
Four names from the bottom of your soul
were sobbed in sleep into the hot hotel room.
Morning brings a consciousness of breathing.
Coffee, or the smell of the lagoon
seem like a shot of meths.
Your chest is skinned and raw.
The still air of the clinic is like smelling salts.
The final treatment raises vowel sounds,
back to the first stirrings of your voice,
and then it stops.
That evening, eating shellfish in a cafe
full of idle conversation, you close
around your quietness. From now on
every word you use is plucked from nowhere.
Everything you say is sudden poetry.

TOPIARY

I LAUREL

When we cut the laurel bush its insects,
shaken from safe darkness, filled the evening
air with bites. Then we discovered its cache
of black-green berries, a secret ripening
behind dark-leaved protecting arms.

By morning, someone had put up a shack
out of the heap of sweet bay branches;
woven in with willow and palm, myrtle and citron.

We had no idea what it was for,
so left it to its gradual dismantling.
And in those days before it dried and fell
children played house in it, we ate in it at night,
and noticed how more stars peered
through the thinning roof, as though a new creation
were beginning piece by piece.

After that our bricks and tiles felt weaker.
Still some nights we wake convinced that rain
strokes down the oil-green leaves
on to our faces, in rooms
containing more air than their walls allow.

Two rows which began as an avenue
were teased to lean, touch, weave,
until immersed in details of each other
they became a back of leaves,
arching in the sun. Within its belly
is a man who came to hide before
the ends grew closed, who slept beneath
the shady lightwood skeleton,
breathing insect plankton, and awoke
too late to leave, inside a deep green whale,
content that somehow,
when its slow swim is complete,
he will be spewed into the daylight
of a distant shore, equipped with all
the words he needs to warn its people.

III SUMAC

Halfway house of flora and fauna,
branches warm with fur, a varnish tree
with beads of russet sap across its pelt
that dry as scarabs –
sumac is easy to climb,
no cross could come of it.
Anti-geometric, it changed tack
with each new arm's length.
Beyond the garden, all gardens,
in a vacant scrub of nettles,
elders, flayed birches;
rude wood is trees becoming,
sows splinters into hands like stigmata.

SCINTILLA

Cradled in my palm this spark
is as cool as it should be hot.
It holds the past and future
in its double-helix, worlds of light:
goldfinch wing-flash in the thorns,
spears that cut through chalk streams,
pyrotechnic blueprint of a phoenix;
and between, shafts of that magenta light
which could be seen as darkness.

THE EEL GATHERERS

Beside the straight road, a disused railway track
which ferried to the front invites you to picture it then.
Beyond that, plump cows print their flanks in Flanders mud.

The eel gatherers finished here and moved
over years and kilometres to wooded valleys split by rivers,
where the lithe ones shin up trees to point out

quick black spasms in the water,
mimicking life's microscopic frenzy,
while the knee-deep scoop them into coracle baskets,

pull them from their blind instinctive journey
– Sargasso, Gulf Stream, Atlantic, then silvering upriver –
into a desperate cross-weave of each other.

DISARMED

When the signal came, it's said they tore
out of the scrubs on horseback,
charged towards their sons and brothers

here on common land, and under
cloudless skies then broke
each others' hearts like butchers.

Old battlefields, civil-war dead
tidied under two grass mounds.
A nation now at peace, but petrified.

New Year's Day, walking on Wash Common,
no one about. Gales like gloved hands
hold us up. The football pitch is sodden,

a walk-in map of undiscovered worlds.
We pick our way across new lands
between new oceans. Clouds

thin the afternoon light from cream
to milk to water. In this wind
the world is skittish, animals in quiet homes

turn wilder, trees reduced to black
are marching. A mile away, Greenham
is getting its Common back.

Fence-bales lie on grass. Gates
are unguarded, silos full of mushrooms,
plugs pulled on the searchlights,

ghost estates of air-force houses.
At nights, short-cutting round the base
we used to catch the faces

of peace women lit by their own
campfires. From that road which was
rubbed out in every atlas you learned

secret landmarks through the fence
– bunkers gestating, cells dividing –
flashing lights like strong blue drinks

which followed you from inside.
Old battlefields. New maps barely hiding
an entropy of fear, plain-clothed,

delicate as pollen in the cold,
in silent planes too high to see,
rehearsing war. In Flanders fields

the farmers still turn bodies
with the earth at ploughing time;
soldiers with soil in their eyes,

earth for eyes, rags for shrouds,
interrupted in the act of vanishing,
empty words in their rictus mouths.

MAPPING THE GENOME

'More delicate than the historians' are the map-makers' colors'
Elizabeth Bishop

The desire to know, to map you to your
bodily soul, not some ghost of a ghost-
in-the-machine; to cross borders,
risk it all for one night, risk this hard-won
equilibrium to know you. A terrible freedom.
There are things it is best not to know,
but then again . . .

Unbuttoning, I chanced upon your own
angelic secret, a hair's-breadth necklace,
a gold halo worn modestly below
the head, warm against your skin.
With the soft consonant of wet lips,
we began a new epistemology of touch.
The sensation of you whispered on my
fingertips for days, the map in my memory
for weeks before details fell away.
Then I wanted to know you again.

OVERSPILL

As children once we broke into a plot of empty houses,
early in the evening when warm light hooded trees,
and flies lagged behind us like birds at a plough.
We tore and echoed round inside then sat upstairs
in silence, waiting to see who would speak.

I thought of that new house as the loss of an old one;
imagined waking on a June day to find nothing
but plaster, concrete, unsanded frames sharp as glass,
looking deep into an overnight hedge enclosing
where lawns had stretched before.

As we left, there were half-melted cattle in the next field,
whose dewlaps swung like famine in the falling light.

LOSING THE LIP

That night the thunder woke you,
you came from a place in sleep so deep
you sat up shocked as Lazarus.
Your page was blank for half a minute,

all you knew was presence; not identity,
nor history, nor me. Like a diver who
comes up so fast her blood begins to boil,
you carried with you properties of dream,

half-formed characters cut loose in
the house like ghosts – a Victorian girl
with mahogany hair and high-lace boots
who watched you through the night,

spiders infesting your pillows,
and the sound of an unplayed flute.
When the flautist lost her embouchure
she lost her kiss as well. They were so close.

No dying cadence, just a glottal stop.
Alone, windows open one hot afternoon,
she settled to practise but her lip
had lost its hard-won instinct,

all finesse was missing. Her fingers
knew it, gentle on their stops and holes.
The birds in the cherry-tree outside
knew it too, and covered for her.

At first she thought the gift had gone.
If given, why not taken? Arbitrary both.
But she felt it was still there,
silent in the numb slug of her upper lip.

Sometimes she, like you, would wake up
in the small hours to discover
pure existence, all her life forgotten.
When she came to her senses she knew

she could have made the lip and played
through that limbo until memory cut in.
Sometimes when drunk she got the embouchure
but lost the fingers. Once in sheer frustration

she snatched a pupil's flute to demonstrate
a phrase and half of it was out before her face
fell and the notes slid into whispers.
Now she keeps a flute by her bed,

hoping the kiss lies in mists and dunes
on the coasts of sleep. She wants to live there,
like sleepers who dream they wake up and go to work,
then wake up and go to work, then wake up.

DRIFTWOOD

That ancient beached oak door
you shouldered home to make
into a straightback chair

left two holes – a sandprint
for the tide to fill, and a dark
hiatus in the deep which swept

astonished shoals from one
sea to another through its needle-eye.
When wet and weed were gone,

the door was too beautiful to break.
It would fit no doorway,
so it leant in the hall for weeks,

until you propped it on two crates,
stood in your coat and ate a meal
off it, then left but left no note.

When you slammed your house shut,
a cold current slid under all
our doors, and every curtain sighed.

QUICKENING

'A fly is a more noble creature than the sunne,
because a fly hath life, and the sunne hath not.'
John Donne

I INCARNADINE

This is love's alchemy, mercurial,
what risk to bring another pair of hands
into the world! A tongue alive with sounds
of long-forgotten gardens, Babel
songs which none can recognise,
wildcat psalms in cedar trees, what risk!
Yet this new life is our elixir,
this soft dividing pearl is our great price.

Incarnadine, vermillion, crimson;
that night your words were made flesh I became
a humming bird trapped in a scarlet room,
whose wings beat so quickly they cannot be seen.

II MIDWIFE

She washes the hands which cradled a head,
which pulled a snipe's shoulders, featherless
wings, roe belly smooth and scale-less,
frogs' legs cocked to jump. She hauls these hybrid
foreigners from one world of light to another,
where they root for words: *milk, white, breast.*
They have come a long way. *I am dressed*
for the journey in a coat of fine lanugo hair.

She washes her hands, the basin swallows
every trace of blood and milky vernix.
This close they could be Pilate's, Herod's fingers,
shaking drops into a rose-water bowl.

III POPPIES

Their red is shut eyes staring at the sun.
They hypnotise – so rich, so violent!
Their translucent beauty is a feint,
lightning strikes you if you touch one.
Resurrection seeds, they double-cross the grave,
fresh among the meat, the chitterlings.
Before the dead turn cold, the quickening
has struck fields red and women heavy.

Born too soon, my loose skin was rice-paper,
veins like tattoos, bones as soft as saplings,
eyelids still sealed shut. I came out howling
in the dark, blindfolded by my maker.

IV MULTIPLICATION

Before I took my name I was as vivid
as colour before cloth, love before lover.
Scrape back the winter's earth to find repair,
a rumoured seed, a plant-beat, gravid.
Deep mathematics of creation:
every hair numbered, every grain of sand.
When the sun's heart caught fire in the mind
of God, heaven gave it no ovation;

but when Eden's river broke its walls,
became a delta, a cacophony of names,
a teeming sea, then every plan and sum
was lost in joy, outstripped by multiples.

V LIVING WATER

It is a charmer's gift, to quicken
water's soul, to stroke a bowl's bronze rim
until a clear note rises from the hum,
ripples turn to waves, to leaps, then light rain
falls from empty skies and sharpens
to a torrent, hail hops like a frog
plague in the scorched fields, and as long
as the note holds, *we dance to its resonance.*

This is water's homage to the Baptist,
who leapt in the womb when Mary called:
Her voice made me kick like a lame man healed,
made me sing like the dumb choirs at Pentecost.

THE STRUCTURE OF GENES

Shaving in the mirror a man may see
his own home in true reverse, its terrible
lack of symmetry, his face the only right-way-round
component of the place, and that a trick of the familiar;
may see ropes of light being lowered to the ground
by summer as it goes home to the sun, and millions
of insects climbing up them.

He may see the risks creation takes with pyrotechnics,
a big bang, a garden, the elements of history
forged by pinpoint use of crushing forces,
ways with fire, massive pressure, rain as though
the sky had melted, ways of handling them
so heat, weight or water will not blow
the start of all he now sees in a square of mercury.
He may see that – the painted silver – but he'd be the first,
he may look at his face and see a tent of bones
he may lean in and see a thin supportive rig of blue wires.

Shaving in the mirror a man may learn that he owns
nothing in his hinterland, may turn to pick a towel
off the door, to find the door turns too, it all does.

Shaving in the mirror a man may see
the whole animate world arrange itself in order,
and leave a space for him, may see
a deep logic of the heart, may see
the patient glove of space a plant must fill,
the slow reports from leaf through stem
that leave dull pulses in the soil.
He may see sense,
he may pull from his jacket pockets two smooth stones:
On one is written 'I am dust and ashes',
on the other 'I am why the world was made'.

WEDDING

It was only when the bride and groom
had left that cool lead crystal showed itself
as withering transparent husks of ice.
As wedding guests spooned out the fruit
their bowls filled up with sunlight,
and began to melt. Some die-hards stayed
to finish all the wine, but no one felt
like talking as the liquifying feast
brought nightfall, pools of saturated berries,
seafood skinned in shallows on the long
wooden tables which warped and cracked
in the gentle final rain. Above the clouds,
spores and seed clocks of a new world
were circling in the hot and rising air.

SALT

'He razed the city to the ground, and sowed it with salt'
Judges 9:45

When snow comes to protect us,
trucks salt cities in a single night –
orange lights pulsing across bedroom walls,
a clatter like hail on parked cars.
At one time, when the massacre was over,
when a city lay shocked in its own entrails,
the victor's men would shoulder
salt-bags, walk the streets, cast
seeds of desolation into corners
where couples used to meet,
seasoning each doorstep with barrenness,
crunching blood and crystals underfoot.

Now once or twice a year we wake
to find our cities overcome.
Children rush to windows
tear back the curtains on silence;
roads splay open like new wounds,
armies are gone into the hills.
Unaware of any battle,
how can we know who defeated us?
How many others were spared
to live like ghosts
beneath their bowed and hooded roofs?

SWIMMING AT GADARA

I

On a hot Saturday the sea
would drain the town of all of us
and leave it for the cats
to cross in unwatched gardens
wild with scent, purple foxgloves
nodding full of bees,
clematis and trellis woven
on the walls, and flies
sewing all together through
the open doors of empty houses.
It was home and destination;
so surely both we could have left it
for a lifetime's swimming,
come back to dry our deep-lined skins,
unable to discern which furrows
were the decades' work,
and which the water's.

II

Each time I grounded from the swim
my feet found ribs of sand and weed,
but just before we left I stood
on sharper ribs like leather,
then plunged through the waterlogged
belly of a pig, its cool centre
where the quick had turned to kelp and oyster.
There was no telling whether more
had fallen from the towering cliffs,
had gorged on sea and settled on its bed.
I started seeing tan hide mounds
beneath my slow crawl to the shore.

If there was a pearl in the oyster,
in the pig, it was the thought
of that Gadarene high on the brink
of his homeland, whose terrors
and regrets were cast into swine
then sea, to boil beneath the surface.
He stood and faced the gales,
heard the waves, felt his bruises
for the first time with the clarity
of one who has travelled so far
from peace that he comes up
behind it again.
So good it was, that he was glad
looking down at the drowning herd,
that all were submerged,
but none was buried.

TENDING THE FLAG

It has always been someone's duty, often an old soldier's,
to haul the flag at dawn up its pole which stakes
this island to the earth through the middle
of its market square, to salute it alone, leave it
to preside over the day then lower and roll it at dusk.

He presses it, dries it, stops the colours bleeding
into one another after rain. When he's gone,
everyone knows nobody will do it.
The flag will soak and blow like forgotten washing,
its rope tap-tapping the pole with an impatient hand.

When cloth drops to threads its barren tree
surrounded by fertility – a starburst of leaves
that change colour by seasons – stands no chance.
A totem of distant, unobservable loyalties.
At night with the flag furled on his kitchen table

he imagines being taken in rapture,
soaring from his garden on a hot afternoon
to look breathless down at the spreading ocean,
to watch his friends uproot the pole and set
their island spinning to collide with continents.

POWER CUT

Men in overalls stood in the basement's odd silence –
not the one rehearsed in lifts before opening,
or phones on hold, but a sprawling dead quiet
from out of town, which grew heavy on the surface of a reservoir
among the hills and slid in through the suburbs leaving
syllable gaps in conversations,
misfires in cars, broken bird arpeggios.

On all floors above, outdoors had crashed in,
no work was possible. Screens that were windows
on that sprawling otherworld of characters and cursors
where this world spends its days were now black tiles.
Hundreds sifted papers under dead-eyed terminals.

Air-conditioning hardware – grand pianos
wrapped in tinfoil – turned stale on the roof.
People had a choice – to breathe each others' air
behind unopenable glass, opaque with blinds,
and make their plans with pens in the dark,
or go out on the streets (their cars entombed underground
by electronic doors) and walk, step out and take
their chances in the wild gases,
feel how pressure changes just before the weather,
see how those poles that look like giant crosses five floors up
look just like streetlights from the pavement.

SPENT

Darkness floats from drifts of Japanese cherry,
brushes the window like eyelashes.
We are splayed on a white bed.
Our scattered clothes are blossomings
of new, exotic trees. A distant baby cries,
but ours are older, and asleep.
Half-awake, we walk into each others' dreams.
My dream moves inside you; crystalline, alive.

In the half-light, we are peat bodies
laid out on museum slabs, flesh tanned
to leather by the sphagnum, sedge;
skeletons collapsed within.
All that remains of our civilisation
is a last wheat meal in our guts,
and a string of twisted sinews round our necks,
which may be noose or necklace.

A NEAR COLLISION OF FREE AGENTS

How were you spared?
Suddenly a motorbike
ticks over by your leg –

it still, you still –
as if posing for a picture,
the bike at boiling-point

as out of place
as a crash-landed satellite
spiked in a meadow,

great waste of speed
translated into vapour
for one massive moment,

buildings on the visor
bowing in thanks
for paths uncrossed.

SMITHEREENS

for James MacMillan

I

Zimzum – before there was light or darkness,
before there was a surface to the water,
before the first breath skimmed on the meniscus,
before there was a vault between
the seas of earth and heaven,
came a single lightning bolt – *Shevira*.

II

My first spark was in snow,
a firefly in an ice-nest, unquenchable
but too dim to transpierce drifts.
I was on a childhood journey
across whole white countries to a new home.

Since the blind are best at leading the blind,
knowing what to look for,
most families let the children run ahead.
I raced to an oleaster tree,
felt the sharp-in-soft contact of my boot
with a shell miles from the sea.
I picked it from the white
and it was fine, translucent, a fragment
of the bone china vessels of creation
smashed by God's let-there-be-light.
Under my shell was a smithereen of sun,
hidden in snow among wild yellow olives.

How to raise it came by instinct.
I cupped the precious relic
in my palms then held it high above my head.
When hands dropped, sky had lightened
by a fraction. Water dripped onto a darker land.

Zimzum, shevira, shattered light
falls as dry rain, static in my hair.

III

I have raised a family in every city
between Kiev and New York.
I have laughed like Sarah,
eaten bread and salt at Esther's banquet.
Like Rachel I have cried and bled for children.
But on sleepless nights of feasts or wars
I have seen above the rooftops
aurora borealis, aurora australis;
northern, southern, eastern, western lights.

Out there, sleeping rough,
someone shakes a blanket and finds
treasure like a jewelled monstrance,
a Prague Sun in among the garbage,
lifts it gently like a nest of bees
to raise a fist of sparks at once,
breaking in the sky and opening eyes.

Zimzum, shevira, shattered light
falls as dry rain, static in my hair.

IV

Many have died in search of these fragments.
Some have tried to make their own, with flint
or electricity. They never lasted.
Some have tried to snuff out sparks with fingers,
and have raised them by mistake,
or swallowed to douse them,
only to find they rise
behind the next unguarded word.
I saw an evil man spit fury,
but his curses came like catherine wheels.

Zimzum, shevira, shattered light
falls as dry rain, static in my hair.

V

Was diaspora for this – to look in places
no one else has looked; to send
the sun home piece by piece?
Still the most elusive are the closest.

I gaze into the eyes of lovers and strangers,
see slide across their irises reflections
of tungsten or the long-angled sun,
the warm shapes of a room in early evening.

The only way to tell an echo from a spark
is to look in utter darkness, and if the gleam
remains find a way of crying tears
so salt-heavy they could wash out a splinter,
and raise a spark as they trickle down.

Zimzum, shevira, shattered light
falls as dry rain, static in my hair.

Despite the sparks still shielded by clay shells,
those that landed far from the epicentre,
those whose disguise is a trivial encounter;
nonetheless the light accumulates.

In a village I once called home
they have saved their last scintilla.
They guard it in its clutch of leaf-mould and worm-casts,
waiting for the world to catch up
so they can raise the last spark of all.

They gather up the firstfruits of their grain,
strip the husks off sunflower seeds,
store the best wine, oil and honey,
honour the girl who discovered the spark
when her knife cut a name in a manna ash,
she who will come back to raise it,
will head the silent line that queues up
by the railway track to welcome its Lord,

as he steps off the last ever train from the north,
as he kisses each one,
as he unties their dead branch backs.

A FREE LUNCH

There is such a thing:
after standing in a quiet house,
unscrewing all the taps
until they jam agape
and puke clear tongues across
striated enamel to the last
wasted string of water:
after exercises in translucency –
in steady bowls like glass,
running like itself
then crossing into air
when that was all the system held –
after draining the house dry,
before unplugging the phone
and following furniture;
eat what was saved
when the fridge was melted,
then leave by a window.

A CALICO COAT

The powerless man wears a calico coat.
It was woven on a water-driven loom.
It was sewn by day and candlelight,
with needles cut from trees and bones.
And in that way no slow electric
seeds were planted in its making,
not even a finger-snap of static.
The powerless man goes tightrope walking,
up between pylons on the slack high wires,
and they hum beneath his shoes,
and in driving rain they fizz.
He strides across fields, across counties,
round the blackened rims of cooling towers,
over the smoke stacks and turbines.
He is safe, he has nothing to lose,
no power can touch or pass through him;
his dead dry coat will not conduct.
At night he buttons up, shins down
to sleep on streets and gather dust,
then scales the angled steel again,
and leaves a nameless sense of loss.

SIBLINGS

for Deborah

When I walk back to my childhood home,
April showers will crack the chestnut leather
shoes my father handed down to me.

I will pass myself off as that missing uncle,
changed by the sea, collar turned on his herringbone
coat in high summer. I will not arrive

first thing, as my father kisses us and leaves,
but just as light is thinning, as my mother
settles us to bed, and wolf-packs hunch

in corners of the room licking last night's wounds,
waiting for the canopy of sleep to make a forest.
My key will fit, despite its rust; I will step

into the hall and hear the lullabies upstairs,
you my newborn sister learning what the dark is for,
as suns become stars in each others' nights.

In my deep coat pockets are presents
from my travels – terracotta worry beads,
beeswax candles that burn down in minutes

but make the house gold and fat as a hive,
pregnant with the sweet hum of the future.
I will lay them on the kitchen table,

along with wine from the year of your birth;
a vintage to drink when our father comes home,
when we babies are asleep upstairs.

I may go up and kiss us both goodnight,
crack the curtains to allow a bar of streetlight in,
and mind the wolves that snap at my heels.

ON DYEING

Once we knew it took a boatful
of crushed shellfish – murex and purpura –
to turn one sleeve imperial purple.
It took millions of beetles to die cochineal,
pulverised madder roots for scarlet,
indigo that went blue when it met the air.
Without mordants to fix them,
all these colours fell to pastel, then to cream.
A dress could drain of lilac in an evening.
No beauty lasted without ox-blood, oil,
oak-galls, urine, alum, salt, shit.
Once we knew the cost of dyeing.

BLOOD-LINES

In a clearing where the last
wild wolf in Britain stepped
into its snare, there is no reek
of blood, no splintered bone,
no hot print in the fallen leaves;
no need. The human babies
she once weaned have raised
whole armies, founded cities,
killed their mother.
Her teeth lie behind their lips.
In that quiet copse hangs
the sugar scent of wolfsmilk.

BOATHOUSE

Like the heart of hearts in a pyramid, death's accoutrements
were laid out there, never meant for the eyes of the living.

Beautiful boats – ten, fifteen, moored in rows
between thin planked jetties – unquestioning, gentle
on ropes like guard dogs trained to the height of obedience.
Esperance, *Branksome*, *Otto*, the air seasoned with old wax
on brass, teak and walnut, all immaculate.
Sounds like dream birds as the moorings rubbed,
and a lapping of water kept indoors.

These were the ferries – steam launches.
They made their journeys slowly in the evenings,
when mountains staggered back in silhouettes
and swans prepared the water for the coming darkness.

These boats have taken all those who commissioned,
named, designed and built them, out across the lake,
some to the island with its circular house,
whose bedroom windows crane above the silver birches,
a haven for those unsure which way to go.
But most outings reached the far shore,
and the launches came back empty through the night.

One summer, someone cut loose this cortège-in-waiting,
set it steamless, aimless out onto the waters.
Tourists and water-skiers watched
as the fabulous craft drifted towards land.
Nobody was sure if it was safe to try
a foot's weight on a deck, a trip towards the island.

As the fisherman said – *'Don't worry, they won't hurt you.'*
They have ferried all their cargo to the other side.
But that far shore's not so distant;
the ice which crusts its shallows has designs on
the whole lake, then slow manoeuvres inland cutting valleys.
Those island birches are rehearsing for a mainland forest.

THE HOSPITALITY OF ABRAHAM

In the heat of the day, builders hammer
roofs to stop them floating off; a gardener
waters ghost-plant fennel, lends it weight,
and as she drains the can it lifts, surprised by lightness.
Rape fields rise like swarms, no bird is flightless.

Since gravity is in this heady state,
I stand and smoke on my verandah, in the shade,
and three identical young strangers come my way.
They have walked for weeks, with more to go.
I say '*Sit beneath my oaks and rest.*' They do.

Under my terebinths, on the cool grass
I bring them water, we kill the best calf.
The triplets wash their feet and hands. We talk
of how this moment came to be, what spans
of time these three had crossed, what unmapped lands.

And in the warm aroma of turpentine bark,
they feed on meat, milk, curds and cake.
They bring us strange gifts – different names,
the promise of a child for our old age –
then leave for Sodom and Gomorrah.

Months from now, with a baby in my arms,
will I rock beneath the heavy leaves, sing songs
of gratitude and terror, of rescue and of loss;
will I try not to see, as my son gapes at the sky,
the thumbprints of smoke from a valley on fire?

The reservoir is parched.
Boats hang halfway up the hills.
Waders slobber, dig with hands or spades,
looking for a crucial plug which somehow
was pulled out, or for some clues
that this is not a drought at all,
but the lifting of a flood, signs of life;

a plough left in mid-furrow,
as though sea had come cascading
down the scree and caught
the villagers off guard. Its blade
has split the same piece of earth
in a field, in a lake, in mud-flats.
Orange with age it tilts towards

a pair of stippled gateposts,
the only drowned left standing.
Like solstice stones they make you line
them up with this horizon point or that,
and usher you from this field into that,
when one is the whole world north of here,
the other south, all hinged on this gate.

On farms across the peaks a bright
corner of a still field in the lee of a barn
is planted as an olive grove or vineyard.
Whole families keep the secret
– that north is moving south –
until evidence is hard enough
black stones on plates, red wine in glasses.

The day Gomer left, she got up before him.
The windows were open. It was high June.
As she swept the front door shut behind her,
all the air in the house rushed out
through the narrowing crack in terror
of hanging around to go stale with Hosea.
The curtains billowed like full sails
on their way somewhere, then sighed flat.

Since then he has never really got up.
His body has. And walked, fed itself,
shopped, even bathed. In the damp footsteps
of Archimedes, Marat, all the greats,
he keeps his seminal events for the bath –
prayers, tuneless whistling, and a look
in bewilderment along his mutineering body,
which while he considers whether
sickness is a part of health,
is telling him under the running taps that
cold water feels like the taste of sugar,
hot water feels like the taste of salt.

ARCHAEOLOGY

Hosea took a chisel to some tiles
to find a fireplace, stripped off wood
and paper, looking for an older home.

He mixed vinegar with water,
took a brush to scrub the moss
and make a surer set of stones to walk upon.

And each morning he shaved,
but the mirror showed the same grim border guard
blocking his way back to other faces.

DIVERS

I saw their wetsuits hunched in grounded boats
like shrugged skins, and new black birds

– neither crow nor chough – watching over them.
Then I noticed the abandoned homes,

stitched with agrimony, gorse-smoke, quitch,
collapsing on the ends of speech.

By the back step of one, an axe had fallen
from the sky into a tree stump. The blow rings

in its rusted head. Touch it and shiver.
The émigrés have gone back to the sea forever,

stripped to subcutaneous blackstrap and weed,
kicking down to the dark seabed.

I found carapace and claws, and rebuilt them
to tempt the crab-souls out again.

SWARMS

In kitchens, on stairs, at dinner tables,
we stood like saints in silent rapture;
upturned faces, raised and open hands.
When we clapped, flies jumped,
riding on draughts out of reach.

Our gardens were primed with foul-scented candles;
jamjar wasp traps full of water –
summer fruit sweetening their lips.

In that swarm season, we never thought
the firstborn of a plague may not be blown in
on the wind, but nurtured close at hand.
Old honey on a high shelf,
hardened into resin, may harbour in vitro
an embossed wing, a breaking leg.

His van crosses cat's eyes into oblivion,
powerless on the hard shoulder.
The glazier zips his jacket shut,
lifts a sample window from the back,
locks and leaves, climbs the verge
under his flat glass umbrella.
Before him: fox in bits, a shoe, tyre-strips,
then over a ridge into woodland,
dense, only yards from this artery
but light years from anywhere at all.
He steps onto the soft leaf matting,
peers up through his window
hoping for spaces in the canopy.
The rain goes straight for his face,
smacking on the new-set glass.
Through his eyes' defensive spasms,
he scans the stars and speaks to them –
'I'll make a deal with you:
watch over me tonight in your time,
and I'll send you back a little
of your faded glory from in mine.'
So he polishes the surface with a sleeve,
angles it to catch the frail light
– so old, so weak from its travels –
and somewhere, if the stars are not
all dead behind their ancient faces,
the glazier knows they will see him
even when he is no longer there to see.
His glass, polished like an instrument,
picks up a trace of rhythmic blue
with no sirens, but it fades out of range –
chasing speeders, not interested in
picking over roadside husks.

SAILBOARDERS

These men wrestle angels. Each now sits on
an enormous wing waiting for the winds to come

which will not come to taunting or to whistles,
just indifference. These gales have flown for miles

across the primeval darknesses of oceans,
fetching up waves, and waves ahead of them.

One gust will animate the faceless imagos,
these giant phosphorescent painted ladies,

send them dancing in a chest-to-chest embrace,
fighting on the beach with a Jacob, an Icarus.

Beyond the chrysalis, they only live one summer,
such is their speed, their coruscating colour.

HISTORY-MAKERS

With fine sable brushes and black
and silver paints, they made
party traitors, mavericks,
self-seekers and the plain bad

vanish from recorded history.
Then when there was no party,
they cleared family albums of thankless
children, wicked uncles, bigamists.

Now they close on the honeycombs
of memory itself. Those kisses
on the inside of my face are brushes.
Landscapes grow empty in my dreams.

WHY WE ARE STILL WAITING

It has been tried before,
in isolated places where a knock
has heralded the risen dead
at the front door,
and some like us have turned the lock
for fear of what the flesh-ghost might have said.

We'd seen ours reach inside
and choke, we'd thumped his back, we'd kissed his life
but still the fishbone hooked his throat,
we knew he'd died.
We mourned – we children, brothers, wife –
then he came back, his shrouds draped like a coat.

And if we'd let him in?
The children thought he'd gone to paradise,
they could not comprehend the dead.
He knocked again,
then padded home on melting ice
through snow, intoning what he might have said.

QUAILS

Beneath the fireworks of parakeets,
finches, cockatiels in aviaries
across the world, the same birds
stalk unnoticed. Endemic,
made of sand and sawdust,
they eat the seed and scraps
spilled from above.
Once, by sheer weight of numbers,
they had a stake in history.
They could sink a ship within sight
of the coast, alighting on mast and sails,
cloud after dark cloud pushing it under.
They could feed an exiled nation,
piling knee-deep miles around the camp,
so starving people had to wade
in still-warm writhing food
to fill their baskets.
Song was bred out of these birds
long ago, so as not to drown
the higher voices. Or at least,
they are keeping a silence in exile.

WIRELESS

(In May 1897, Marconi sent the first radio message across water, from Lavernock in South Wales, to Flat Holm in the Bristol Channel. The message was the letter 'S')

'S', hiss, primal sound, default letter
from which all speech, music, books were born,
dot-dot-dot, morse for white noise.
The first trip radio made over water
carried as its luggage 'S'; waves across waves
it told the sea a story in its own voice,
a tale of water on a shingle beach.

★

In hyperspaces between stations,
radio reverts to sibilance, to 'S',
the universal broadcast of a plural.
Maybe Marconi was weaned on a word
made to be whispered – *sarsaparilla* –
dark juice of underground forced up
on a breath between palate and tongue.

★

'S' in morse without 'O' 'S'. Save, just
save – he was too uncertain of his soul.
Does radio have a half-life, weakening
as it loops and loops the world?
Somewhere in a dripping cave where wireless
goes to die, Marconi's 'S' curls like a paper
message washed out of its bottle.

★

Obsolete distress calls dumped by radio
waves in rock pools glow like ripe
cherry anemones. I fished some out
and held against my ear the faded maydays,
tragic as Titanic luggage, unpacked
now by scientists, silk and lace falling
from their folds like shimmering spirits.

★

White roses as sensitive as crystal sets,
planted at the end of each row of vines.
If there's a sickness in the air, roses will
fall first, and precious champagne grapes
are sprayed and netted. So it was
with the earliest receivers.
They would catch a voice and die with it.

★

Marconi's voice: *sarsaparilla was my first,*
waterglass my last, but I will keep
one more 'S' back, so when my tomb
is unsealed I will hiss
through parchment lips and then my face,
my origami death mask,
will be shocked to dust by open air.

★

Wildtrack – radio with no voices, music,
codes, the sound of unmarked canvas.
At the end of each recording, thirty seconds'
nothing, a shared stillness. Actors,
audiences, engineers all honour it
because the dumb deserve a hearing,
and wireless always ends in silence.

THE SHORTEST DAY

In spite of ice, pulse is everywhere
this morning in the dead of December –
crows that walk the high wires,
old trees dragging at the soil,
our baby's gentle fontanel.

And as I'm holding him, the sun
– contracted to a burning coin –
starts dancing in the room for us.
Caught by my watch-face, it spells
the baby's name across the wall.

We splash in pools of sun like puddles.
Dark forms dive and surface
as we pair with shadows.
This is play for the incarnate,
even angels are denied it.

On the twelfth floor a man was making good
the filigree stair-rails. His work curled up
through the hotel. In every crevice he pressed
and brushed quivering leaf tissues,
as thin as top skin sheen on koi carp,
now a little colder in their tanks, a little
less reflective. Flakes of burnish fell across
the carpet, snow from a baroque heaven.

By morning he had gilded his way
to my super-heated room on the thirteenth.
Outside, where hotels face up to the great lake,
there was ice on roads and in the air;
and people who had slept out there said:
*'How about some money, you've been sleeping
in a warm room.'* All day I carried in the tread
of my boot a grain of gold, like a trademark.

SHASH

Not the luminescence after 'Off' but the black-and-burst patterns
of naked television when the shows have gone.
Picked up in the home at night it mesmerises like a fire,
and just as in the hearth we may contain
the element which could provide our end;
so on that screen a chance to study, tanked-up, safe,
the end of all communication, ultimate rhetoric, dissolution.

I turn off the lamps and let it dance into the room – electric snow,
a shredder which pulps images and words into white noise.
Out and above grows a belt of dead signals like a second sky.

DECEMBER HOAR FROST

When sunlight cut the white day
hard and low, when marble berries
turned to blood, when trees
shivered free of ecstatic trances,
when the multiple chimes of thaw began,
when gardens and rivers were febrile again;
the new year which had fattened
on nothing, like fish under ice,
broke the surface with an open mouth,
which may have been gold or rust.

ULTRAMARINE

for Philip Archer

Looking for the perfect blue,
water to swim in, not through,

to fill his sea, his massive bowl
of hand-thick bronze which should hold

more than light (its dozen
compass-pointing bearer oxen

braced in constant expectation)
Solomon scoured every nation

for a colour that was right.
Now and then he would catch sight

of utter blue as he bent down
in some remote spice-scented town

to wash a day's heat from his face,
but when he moved the dish – no trace.

If water needed autumn's slant,
the market traders' day-long chant

a smell of orange, sandalwood
elusive as the blue in blood

then he would reproduce it all –
and this was wisdom. Some would call

it waste, a bad example;
some will never build a temple.

STILLS

for Martin Bence

I

Entering the dark-room to start work,
you found a thermometer in halves,
under inches of water in the sink.

Its marrow lay as silken, misted
spider's-egg-sac drops of mercury,
essence of monochrome, cinnabar soul.

Already lacking clocks or daylight,
this windowless room had no measure or bounds
from the moment the silver left the glass.

II

An overbrimming pewter bowl of fruit,
bruising with weight, bellying airless below,
where skins purse into lips and colours run.

The house fills with liquor scents that say,
'Here's proof of patience from trees seen as barren.'
It's a fragrance from the borders of life and death,

strong and sweet to revive or embalm,
like the smell of spikenard in Lazarus' house,
which lingered for weeks on his sister's hair.

Dead things. Flowers like frost aberrations.
Empty seed pods. Scissored scallop shells.
Insects pinned to trays. A rat's skull like a bird's,

the white beak hidden in its nose all along.
It could have been the skull of that moorhen
caught among the rushes in an endless plunge.

You fished it out to take a photograph.
It looked utterly broken, splayed on the bank,
and yet only missing some scintilla.

IV

In glass-fronted cabinets of static flight,
a kestrel hovers by a hummingbird,
an arctic tern takes a vertical dive.

Pull focus and the bystanders appear
reflected in the glass. Less substantial
than the ranks of the stuffed. It is as though

time among the living has been frozen
to allow the long-dead and waiting
to fill their lungs, arch their backs, and wait some more.

V

Setting out a still-life on the floorboards,
and light pokes in through the tree outside your window.
Playing resurrection with the objects, with shadows

of the breezing leaves, it's saying *'See that lemon*
spiralling its peel back round itself,
the butterflies and wasps warm waking,

these are all the seeds of animation.'
Then just as quick the light left them for dead,
then back to make the fish swim on its plate.

FIRST THINGS

First; laying ground rules like the cook
who said she would skin any meat but hare
because once they lost their pelts
they had a look of newborn babies.
Or children let loose first on the plaster
of undecorated walls, so their pictures
lay behind the paper as a blueprint
for every encounter in that room.

And in particular Saint Patrick, who knew
a thing or two about first things,
and claimed the soil for each new church
by scratching with his staff the alphabet.
Literacy, culture, the very word was made
of these. No wonder Saint Columba
ate a cake with every letter cut, for fear
he may forget them, which would be a last thing.

CAT'S EYE

There was a scramble for mementoes when the road
across the border was smashed up, and there was no
way in or out of this province of great lakes
and mountains. High on a terraced garden,
where potatoes and carrots have begun to replace blooms,
a broken cat's eye lies in its hand-sized
block of rusted iron, and blinks at the house lights
every night unseen. Close up, it's like a toad
with ivory leather skin, run over countless times
but each time shrugging back into its shape,
with eyes in the back of its head, two deep sockets
facing either way and only one glass marble
left for each direction. Who will explain this
when the cars have been melted, when all roads
are rocky paths and scree slopes, when silent boats
cross lakes at night by moonlight only? Imagine
two old friends in darkness years from now,
snaking up the garden steps with ancient
petrol lighters, to try to trick the cat's eye into waking.

NOTES

'Smithereens' is based around a Hasidic Jewish story of creation and redemption, which came to my notice in a work called *The Light of the Eyes*, by Rabbi Menahem Nahum of Chernobyl (1730–97).

The story depicts God holding back his power and light to make space to create something other than himself, an act of self-limiting or withdrawal called *Zimzum*. Then into that space God shines his light of creation, but that light is so intense that is smashes the clay vessels intended to capture it – a cataclysm known as *Shevira*.

This cataclysm results in fragments of divine light – sparks – being scattered across the world, landing in accessible and inaccessible places. Sometimes these sparks are concealed by shards of the clay vessels.

The purpose of life then becomes a redemptive one, to find and raise the sparks, and make the divine light complete again. According to Hasidic teaching, these sparks may lie in trivial encounters or major challenges. They are as likely to be found in the eyes of strangers as those of your own children.

This creation and redemption story has a dark twin in the chilling parallels – broken vessels, shattered light falling – between Chernobyl's Hasidic tradition and its twentieth-century infamy.